ROUGH
interiors

Sibylle Kramer

ROUGH
interiors

BRAUN

CONTENTS

PREFACE

Rough interiors – this term denotes buildings and rooms that at first glance seem to shun perfection and focus on the existing elements and structures. This book combines 55 multifaceted projects – from low budget concepts to luxury space. Despite their great variety, they have one thing in common – the existing substance was creatively incorporated into a consistent design concept. What makes these rough interiors so fascinating? After all, they are all located inside rooms or buildings that once served another function and had long since abandoned or neglected. The spaces were no longer modern, were considered outdated or economically no longer viable and frequently lost in oblivion. After their conversion, they were rediscovered and revived "sleeping beauties." Similar to the fairytale princess who was kissed awake by the prince, they underwent a substantial transformation. The new designs combine

highly contrasting old and new materials and sometimes entire rooms are inserted like an implant into existing structures.

The special attraction for people working and living in these spaces is certainly the joy of discovery. It almost seems as if the history and stories associated with the buildings continue to be seen, heard and experienced in the new rooms. At the same time, one of the strengths may be the simplicity and understatement, the (re)focus on the essential and original. The imperfect substance is not considered a deficit but a chance to focus on the essential. This approach seems to be particularly palpable in the challenge between old and new. The traces of history on the wall are not hidden behind uniform and standardized walls, but remain visible in their uniqueness rendering them readable like the works of the Old Masters. The rooms and structures tell

The patina of real-life history is unique and irreplaceable.

of their history, enhancing the environment of the new users. This results in peerless spaces that serve a great variety of purposes – ranging from popular and hip restaurants, via vacation homes to modern and innovatively laid out offices spaces. It is thrilling to see how well these old and often solidly built walls can be adjusted to the contemporary requirements of comfortable living. Of course, architects and designers do not make any concession when it comes to the furnishings, instead utilizing the old structures as the basis for creating a dialog between the future and the past, resulting in visible frictions at the contact areas and points, which is why these interiors are perceived exactly as they can be called – rough. The patina of real life history is unique and irreplaceable, and each one of these matchless projects cannot be copied even

with large degrees of architectural skills and creativity – a clear indication that these spaces primarily fulfill the contemporary desire for authenticity. Incompleteness is elevated into a principle, the new architecture is encapsulated like an implant inside the protective cover of the surrounding environment to be discovered and virtually peeled out by the user, it is the living core inside an evolved casing. Just like in the fairy tale, the sleeping beauty is hidden behind somewhat reluctantly accessible and apparently repellent brambles of thorns. Similar to the fairy tale prince, the designers of the projects gathered here have succeeded in a key task – to recognize the sleeping beauty of each location and to transform it. Allow their efforts to also kiss you awake!

RUSTY

RAW

RESTRUCTURED

ROUGH

interiors

RUGGED

REJUVENATED

RAGGED

REVIVED

GMOA CELLAR

What is the best way to expand a 1858s
establishment without destroying its charm?

The answer is a contemporary uncluttered dining area inviting guests to sit at tables covered in white tablecloths to discover the excellent Viennese cuisine and enjoy their wine, while offering regular customers wooden and classical Formica tables to drink their beer. With a few simple steps, the room can be converted into an event venue. No playful decorations were used and the brick vault was whitewashed to avoid any touch of romantic wine-cellar ambiance. Classical pubs make do without ventilation pipes. The installed ventilation required for the underground room is invisible to the guests. The timber floors and wall paneling are stained in a dark hue. The curtain, installed on a theater curtain rail, can divide the room into zones and structure the large vault with recesses.

Architects | Sue Architekten ZT GmbH
Project address | Am Heumarkt 25, 1030 Vienna, Austria
Original use | tavern
Completion of existing building | 1858
Function today | tavern
Completion of conversion | 2010

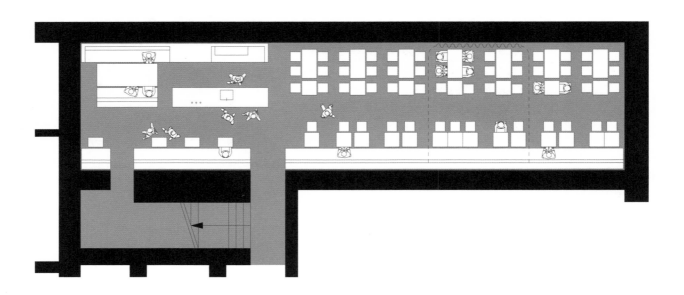

The Waterhouse was built into an existing Japanese Army headquarters building from the 1930s. The architectural concept behind the renovation rests on a clear contrast of old and new. The original concrete building has been restored while new additions built over the existing structure using Cor-Ten steel, reflecting the industrial past of this working dock at Huangpu River. The interior is expressed through both a blurring and inversion of the interior and exterior, as well as between the public and private realms. The public spaces allow one to peek into private rooms while the private spaces invite to look out at the public areas, such as the corridor windows overlooking the dining room. These visual connections not only bring an element of surprise, but also confront the guests with the local urban area.

THE WATERHOUSE AT SOUTH BUND

Expect the unexpected: This five-star boutique
hotel surprises with the mind-blowing combination
of shabby and classy. A jewel of renovation at the
new Cool Docks!

Architects and interior designers | Neri&Hu Design and Research Office
Project address | Maojiayuan Road No. 1–3, Huangpu District, Shanghai 200011, China
Original use | Japanese Army headquarters
Completion of existing building | unknown
Function today | boutique hotel
Completion of conversion | 2010

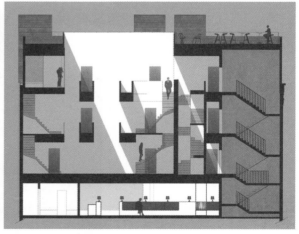

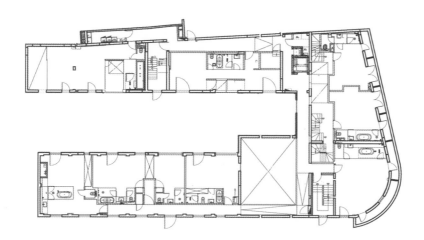

BUTCHER'S SHOP BAR

From meat to Martini. The combination of old tiles and new wooden surfaces transforms the former butcher shop into a classy bar.

Architects | Michael Grzesiak THEZIMMER
Project address | Jahnallee 23, 04105 Leipzig, Germany
Original use | butcher shop
Completion of existing building | 1865, 1901
Function today | bar
Completion of conversion | 2012

The design juxtaposes the existing esthetic density consisting of tiles, panels, and a colorful glass ceiling, with a new and self-confident shape system. This is limited to powerful yet understated timber shapes. The wood intercepts the cold atmosphere of the tiled rooms, providing patrons with warm touchable surfaces made of oak, ash and pear tree wood. The expansive counter is covered in "oak tiles" in various thicknesses, while the long bench consists of a linear ash batten and the pedestal is covered in pear wood parquet. The sideboard behind the bar is made of dark red melamine resin boards that add a pleasant and lightly colored touch to the green ornamental tiles and black tiled panels.

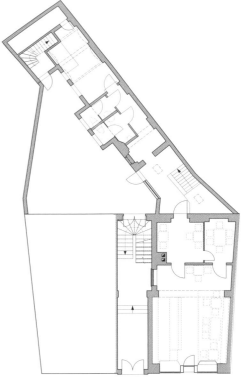

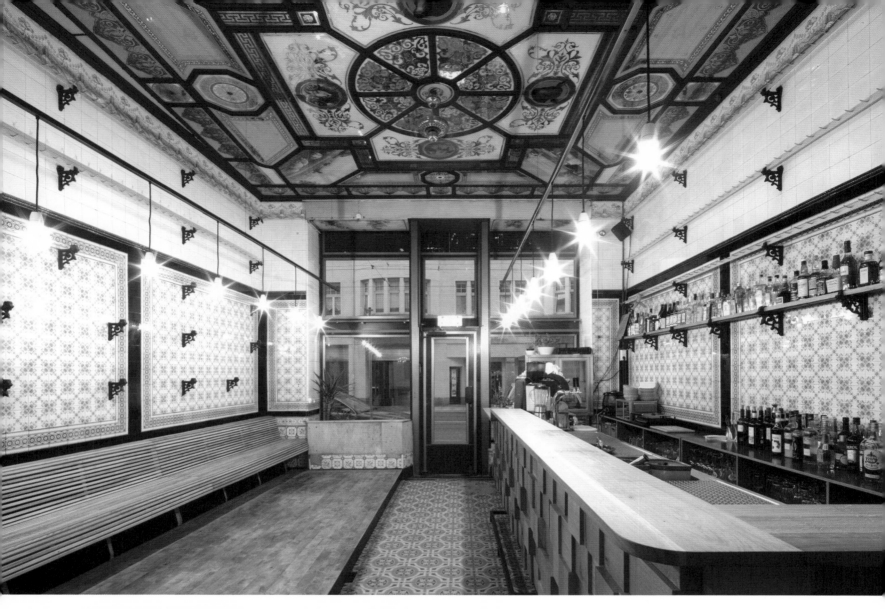

Astley is a site rich in historic resonance – a moated castle, lake, church and the ghost of pleasure gardens. The castle walls decayed and collapsed after a fire in 1978 and a series of rescue attempts failed. A new house was constructed within the oldest part of the castle, building new walls directly onto existing remains, and retaining wings from the fifteenth and seventeenth centuries as walled external courts. The structure occupies roughly half the footprint of the ruins, while new lintels, walls and beams across the courts tie and buttress the retained fragments into a coherent and stable whole. Witherford Watson Mann opted to maintain the open character of the ruin rather than attempt to recreate the castle's former completeness. Every room is a dialog of construction across the centuries.

ASTLEY CASTLE

Like phoenix from the ashes: The concept of a luxury holiday residence salvages the ruins of the medieval castle.

Architects | Witherford Watson Mann Architects
Client | the Landmark Trust
Project address | Astley, near Nuneaton, Warwickshire, UK
Original use | castle, converted to hotel, ruined after a fire in 1978
Completion of existing building | 11th–20th centuries
Function today | holiday house
Completion of conversion | 2012

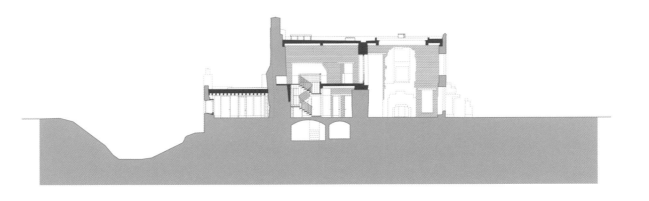

E+M 53

53 m² of democratic space. A synthesis of everything that is needed.

Architects | estudoquarto
Project address | Brescia, Italy
Original use | residential building
Completion of existing building | 1957
Function today | residential building
Completion of conversion | 2009

The space was freed from constraints and disruptions and evenly spread out to enhance the void. The central element is the synthesis of everything that is needed – a kitchen and a bathroom, and the most functional lighting fixtures. The choice of four noble materials: stone, wood, iron and glass for the entire space simplifies the means of expression, removing what is not essential, creating a foundation for merging the house with the experience of life in general. The chosen materials define the project. The elements, always natural and never contrived, express the architectural idea of a transition from "comprehensive" to "partial". Ancient and modern materials give an important signal: focusing on the essence of things and on basic needs, mixing primordial materials and high technology.

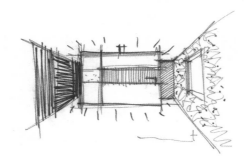
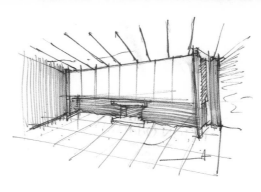

33

LECTURE BUILDING WEICHENBAUHALLE

From steel works to mind works. In a hall where railroad switches were previously manufactured, today university students are educated.

Architects | giuliani.hönger, Dipl. Architekten ETH BSA SIA
Project address | Fabrikstrasse 6, 3012 Bern, Switzerland
Original use | workshop for track and switch construction
Completion of existing building | 1915
Function today | lecture building
Completion of conversion | 2010

The spatial organization of the new lecture center is based on the concept of a building within a building, which allows the creation of attractive lecture halls and distinguished foyer spaces that serve as intermediate climate zone, and the integral preservation of the existing bearing structure and building envelope. Old and new structuring elements coexist in a multifarious, identity-shaping spatial composition. The daylight openings provide visual connections between the lecture hall and the foyer as well as between the exterior and the interior spaces, creating a variety of spatial connections. These vistas result in a kaleidoscope of spaces, which come together in an assembly of old and new structures.

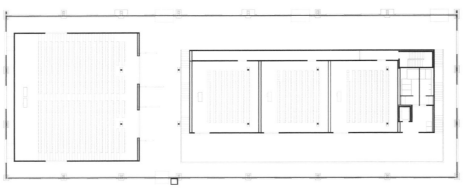

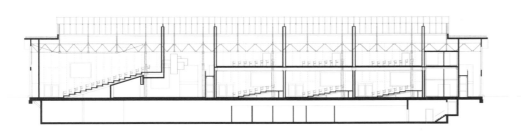

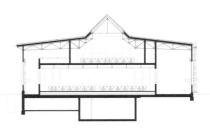

Due to its enormous height, a large part of the inner volume of the hall remained unused. Groosman Partners doubled the usable surface of the halls by adding an extra floor. This idea was derived from the unused crane tracks that demonstrated their carrying capacity before. The extra loading capacity is used to "hang" new functions in the structure. The office unit, designed as a steel structure with a light and flexible fill-in, is attached to supporting beams in between the crane tracks. The suspended floor coinciding with the existing construction is kept open to exhibit the industrial structure. The underside of the office is covered with a satellite image of the port of Rotterdam. This first unit can be connected to a future system of gangways leading to additional units.

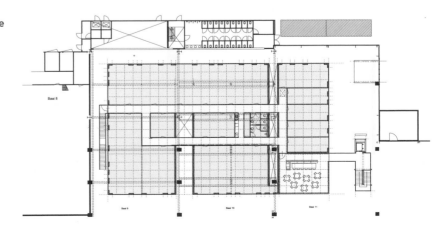

38

RDM INNOVATION DECK

Office facilities in a former machine hall. Very innovative: the space is doubled by plug-in modules.

Architects | Groosman Partners Architects
Project address | RDM-kade, Rotterdam, The Netherlands
Original use | machine hall, part of the Rotterdam dry-dock company
Completion of existing building | 1910
Function today | campus for education and innovation
Completion of conversion | 2012

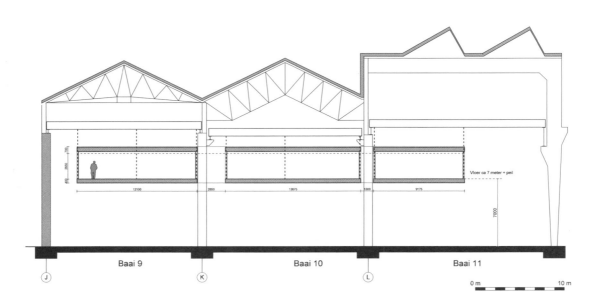

Baai 9   Baai 10   Baai 11

Ⓙ   Ⓚ   Ⓛ

0 m   10 m

40

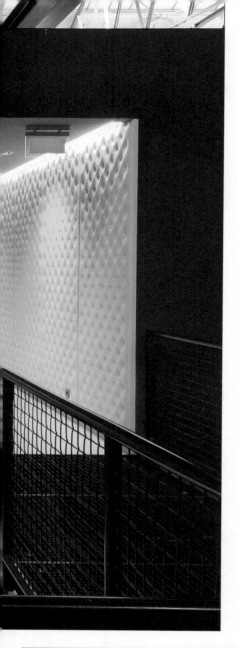

SEMPLA HEADQUARTER

Remembering the industrial past while working in a
modern office. An urban landscape in miniature.

Architects | DAP studio / elena sacco-paolo danelli
Project address | Corso Regio Parco n. 15, Turin, Italy
Original use | factory for the production of cables
Completion of existing building | 1925
Function today | information technology company
Completion of conversion | 2012

The architects decided to crystallize and preserve the traces of the old factory and its
degradation, enhancing the contrast between new and old. The layout is not based
on the conventional design of the workstation, i.e. chair-and-desk, but rather on
the construction of relations. Some functions – private offices, break area, meeting
rooms – are included in new volumes that are placed freely within the perimeter of
the factory. These white elements have simple forms and different heights, keeping
the industrial building always perceptible in all its strength. The dialogue between
the remnants of the factory's past and the new identity marks the passage from the
industrial world to the advanced tertiary economy, representing the transformations
underway in the city of Turin and elsewhere.

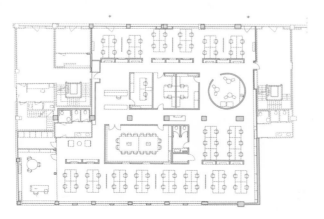

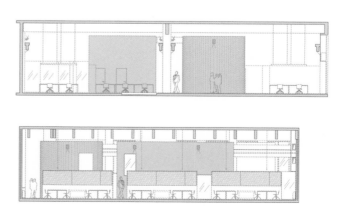

45

FORTRESS OF FORTEZZA

Minimum, yet targeted intervention establishes the dialog between the historic structures and contemporary architecture.

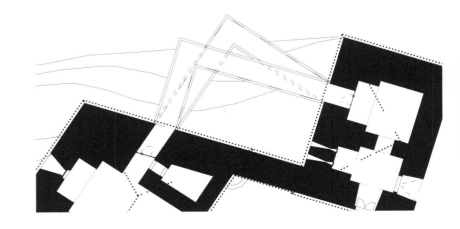

Architects | Markus Scherer Architekt with Walter Dietl
Project address | Franzensfeste, Italy
Original use | fortress
Completion of existing building | 1838
Function today | exhibition spaces and function rooms
Completion of conversion | 2009

The fortress consists of a top, middle, and lower level, while its approximately 20 hectares of floor space make it the largest fortress of the alpine region. The former defense structure was turned into a venue for interaction and cultural exchange. The basic concept was to keep the original state intact and to make the fortress usable with minimum intervention. The patina and aura of the fortress remain in sync with the measures for development and new use. A limited number of carefully selected elements create new connecting paths and can be used as exhibition spaces. Locally available materials were chosen. The color scheme and materials create "abstract" links to the existing architecture, yet clearly distinguish the new additions.

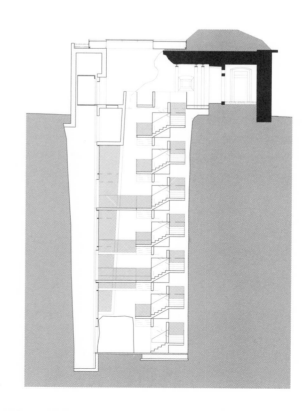

KIRCHPLATZ OFFICE AND RESIDENCE

What a makeover – natural daylight and a crisp
white finish convert the historic farmhouse into an
elegant office and residence.

Architects | Oppenheim Architecture + Design and
Huesler Architekten
Project address | Kirchplatz, Muttenz/Basel,
Switzerland
Original use | farmhouse
Completion of existing building | 1743
Function today | office building, residence
Completion of conversion | 2011

The converted farmhouse received a fresh interpretation of its existing traditional
features and interior. This was achieved by creating new openings for natural daylight
and by using a crisp white finish for the interiors, which juxtapose against the texture
of the old wood, as well as the way in which the spaces open up, overlap, and merge
with one another. Today the building serves as an office for an architectural design
company, with a community meeting space and a compelling link to a new, adjacent
private residence. This elegant contemporary residential structure juxtaposes with
the historic building. The new and old share common materials and colors yet have
distinctly different expressions with interplay of modern and historic elements that
delights the senses.

The expansive premises of the former brewery present a magnificent example of early 19th century industrial architecture. The 6,500-square-meter underground vault system is as impressive as the yellow-red brick façades. After being partially destroyed in World War II, the plot lay abandoned in a state of neglect. Based on the overall concept by van geisten.marfels Architekten, the buildings are now respectfully restored and restructured according to the guidelines for historical monuments. In addition to La Soupe Populaire, the premises will house a hotel, cultural institutions and other dining establishments. The project is a prime example of an urban mixed use, constituting a symbiosis of cultural, residential and commercial utilization.

LA SOUPE POPULAIRE

A liaison of art and culinary excellence. Gourmet chef Tim Raue opened his new restaurant deep in the heart of Berlin, on the premises of the former Bötzow brewery.

Concept | Wunderblock Berlin
Furniture | Luis Mock
Project address | Prenzlauer Allee 242, 10405 Berlin, Germany
Original use | brewery
Completion of existing building | 19th century
Function today | restaurant and exhibition space
Completion of conversion | 2013–2019

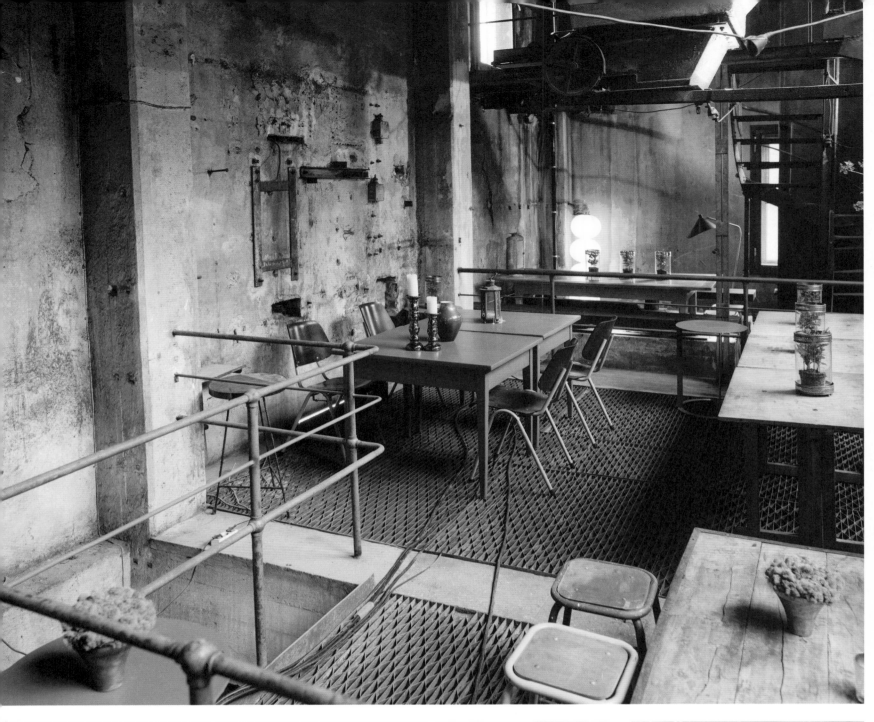

OLD

OBTUSE

OBLIQUE

ROUGH

OUGH

interiors

OPTIMAL

OBSTRUSIVE

ORIGINAL

Situated within the prestigious Three on the Bund, Mercato is Shanghai's newest
culinary destination. Neri&Hu's design for the 1,000-square-meter restaurant draws
not only from the chef's culinary vision but also from the rich historical context of its
locale, which harkens back to Shanghai of the early 1900s, when the Bund was a bus-
tling industrial hub. Stripping back the strata of finishes that have built up after years
of renovations, the design concept celebrates the beauty of the bare structural
elements. Three on the Bund was the first building in Shanghai built out of steel, and
the architects' decision to reveal the original steel columns pays homage to this
extraordinary feat. New insertions are clearly demarcated against the textured
backdrop of the existing brickwork, concrete, plaster, and moldings. Constantly
playing the new against the old, Neri&Hu's design is a reflection of the complex
identity of not only the historical Bund, but of Shanghai at large.

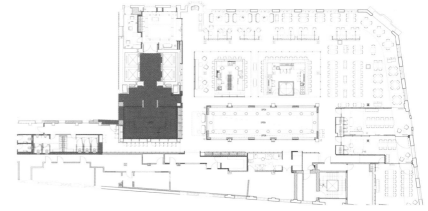

MERCATO

Three star dining? Three star design!

Architects | Neri&Hu Design and Research Office
Project address | 6th floor, Three on the Bund, Shanghai, China
Original use | office building
Completion of existing building | 1916
Function today | hospitality, restaurant
Completion of conversion | 2012

RENOVATION OF AN OLD BARN

A meeting place, a project, a 17th century barn, and a cultural highlight. Conveying the passion of the location that combines the highlights of the countryside and its cultural heritage.

Architects | Comac
Project address | Charroux 03140, France
Original use | barn
Completion of existing building | 17th century
Function today | restaurant
Completion of conversion | 2012

With a humble and respectful attitude, the building was freed from its confining walls and structural skeleton to interfere gently with the space. Two sections, the kitchen and the dining room, made of wooden supports, were isolated, strongly braced and coated with plywood, and positioned opposite from each other. Consisting of a wooden deck and connecting the inside to the outside, the openings of the volumes expand the different openings of the barn letting the area continue from the restaurant towards the terrace, which is the only intervention visible from the street.

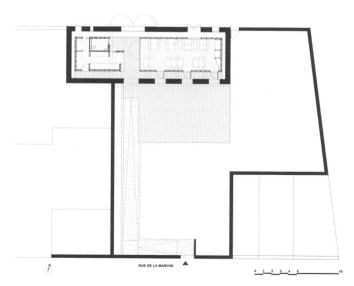

RUE DE LA MARCHE

0 1 2 3 4 5   10

UNIVERSITY OF THE ARTS

Be inspired... The perfect place for studying arts.

Architects | Rolf Mühlethaler Architekt BSA SIA
Art and Construction | Mona Hatoum
Client | Bau-, Verkehrs- und Energiedirektion des Kantons Bern, represented by Amt für
Grundstücke und Gebäude
Project address | Fellerstrasse 11, 3027 Bern, Switzerland
Original use | Schild fabric factory
Completion of existing building | 1960
Function today | university of the arts
Completion of conversion | 2008

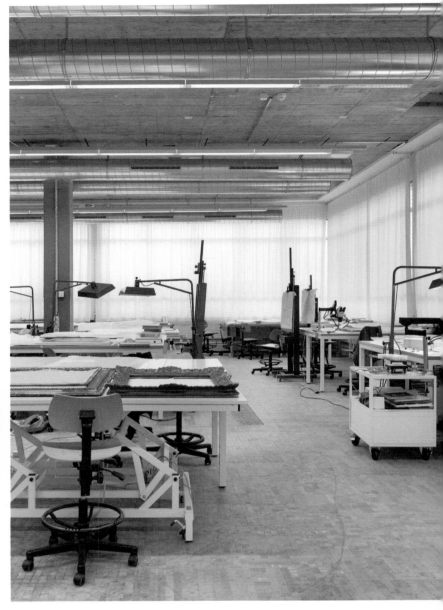

The trilogy of floors, each with very different structural and spatial divisions as well as illumination themes, represents the external and internal identity and logic of the multi–floor factory. The names of the large access and orientation spaces, "factory lane" and "shed hall", are clearly connected to the architecture and the building's old and new uses. A respectful dialog between old and new, coupled with an unbiased critical continued use of the advantageous aspects of the generously proportioned building aims to establish an unparalleled authenticity. The spirit of the industrial building lives on.

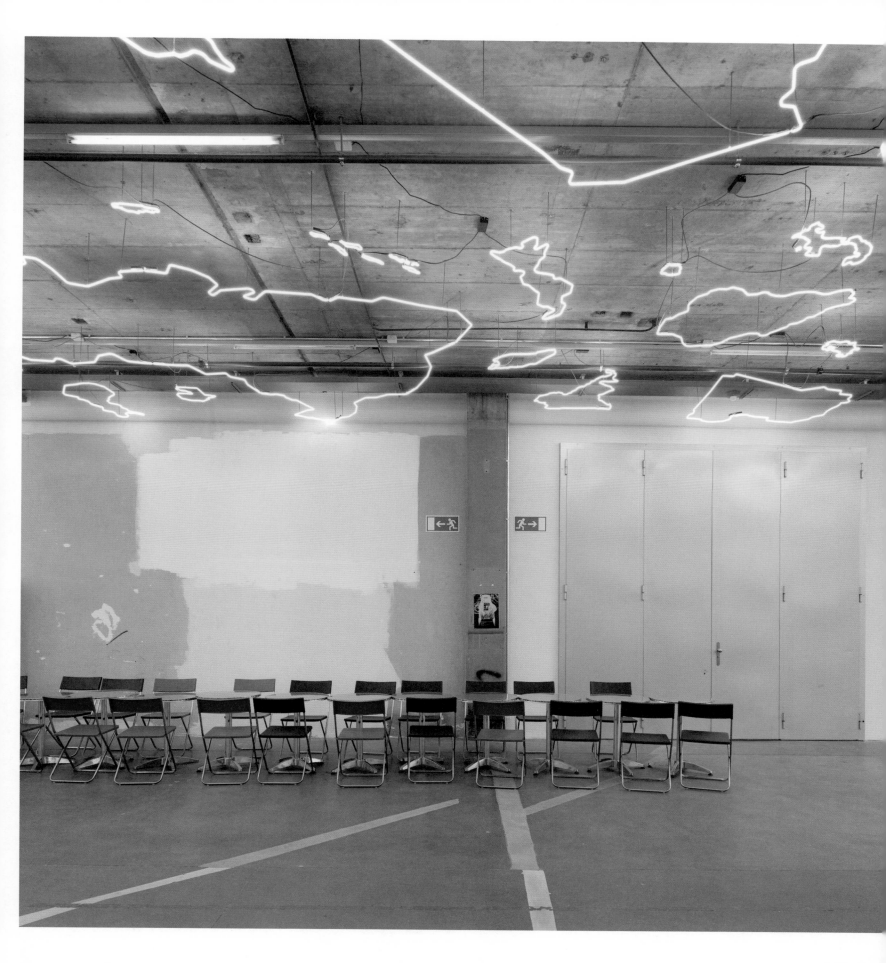

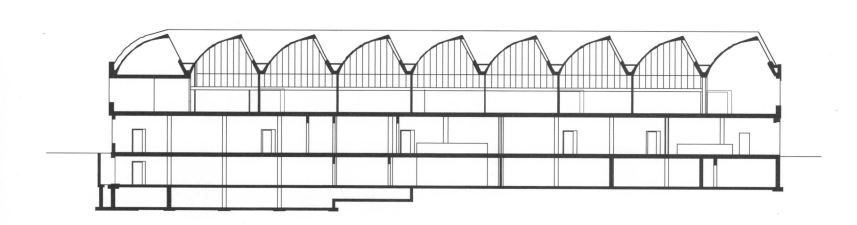

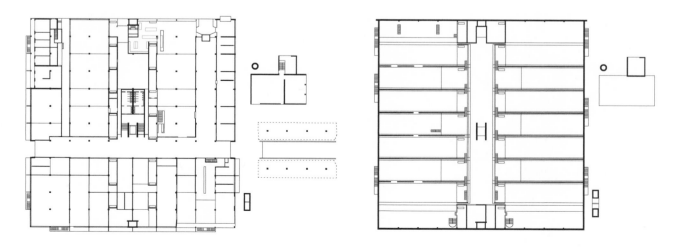

WAREHOUSE SPEICHERSTADT

Everybody loves Hamburg's warehouse charm...

The R2 warehouse was constructed in 1905 and is part of Hamburg's Speicherstadt district that was put under architectural monument protection in 1991. The warehouse consists of a basement and seven warehouse levels. The historic use as a warehouse was discontinued and modern offices were created. The ground floor level includes a special exhibition area. The gentle handling of the existing structure of the building and the preservation of the visible architectural structures, coupled with the conversion of the previous storage areas into modern offices distinguish this restructured former warehouse.

Architects | SKA SIBYLLE KRAMER ARCHITEKTEN
Client | HHLA Hamburger Hafen- und Logistik AG
Project address | St. Annenufer 2, 20457 Hamburg, Germany
Original use | warehouse
Completion of existing building | 1905
Function today | office, showroom, dining area
Completion of conversion | 2013

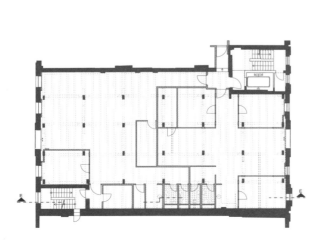

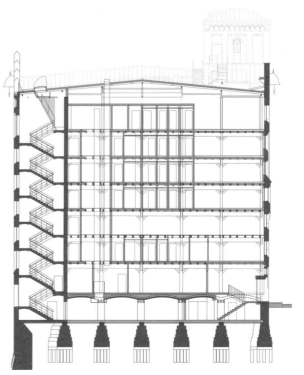

HAKA RECYCLE OFFICE

The beauty of garbage: A colorful, simple and eco-friendly "Living Lab"!

Architects | DOEPEL STRIJKERS
Project address | Vierhavensstraat 38, Rotterdam, The Netherlands
Original use | industrial building
Completion of existing building | 1932
Function today | office building, campus for clean-tech activity
Completion of conversion | 2010

Doepel Strijkers was asked to develop a concept for the ground floor that transfers the concept of material cycles on a city scale to the interior of a building. Waste materials from demolition sites and waste products from production processes were harvested, transported, and processed in the HAKA building to form the new interior elements. However, the ambition was to go further than just reducing the CO_2 footprint through the reuse of materials. An alternative development was set in place by introducing a social component. A team of ex-convicts in a reintegration program was employed in the making of the objects. In so doing, the project is more than just an example of how one can make an interior from waste, as it creates added value through empowerment and education.

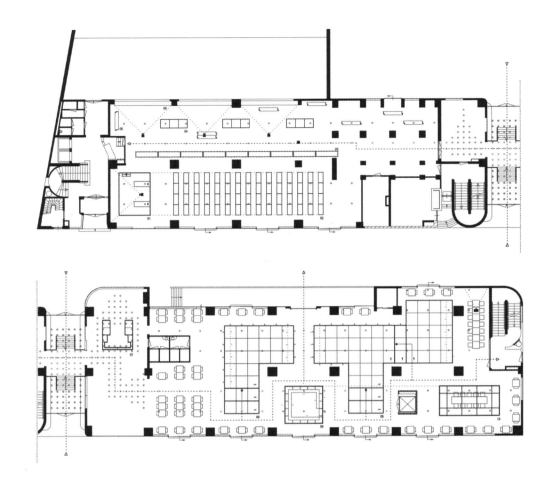

BAKER D. CHIRICO

A breadbasket the size of a shop. A basket that is
also a rack. A single gesture.

Architects | March Studio
Project address | 178 Faraday Street, Carlton,
Melbourne, Australia
Original use | DVD shop
Completion of existing building | unknown
Function today | bakery
Completion of conversion | 2011

Bread is a simple product, with few ingredients, traditionally displayed and sold in
a plain manner. At artisan Baker D. Chirico in Melbourne, March Studio created an
interior with a simple purpose: to cool the bread fresh out of the oven, and to display
it free of packaging and ready to be portioned and sold. An undulation of CNC-
routed plywood forms wall and ceiling. Subtractions from the wall provide display
areas for bread, with the varying depths of the shelves and heights of the dividers
meticulously arranged to accommodate long baguettes, large round pagnotta, ficelle
loaves and other bread creations. The variety and expanse of the wall gives freedom
to arrange and alter the display according to mood or season. Rather than drawing
influence from style or fashion, the design of the interior is an extension and visual
representation of the baking process.

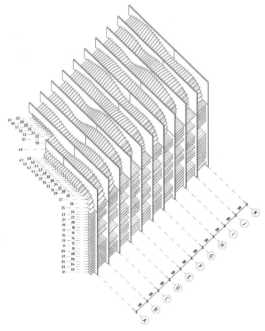

.HBC RESTAURANT & BAR

Mixing history, architecture, and coolness –
contemporary Berlin at its best!

The redevelopment of the restaurant and bar in the former Hungarian cultural institute at the Alexanderplatz in Berlin boasted a unique and imaginative approach to the location's history, architecture, and geography. unit-berlin was asked to completely redesign the dining area, bar and "tower room". This resulted in a design of stark contrasts and a very special atmosphere that is typical of contemporary Berlin. Particularly prominent are the concrete-globe lamps, which were inspired by the location's character. The lamps are freely suspended and can, much to the surprise of the guests, suddenly begin to swing, leaving visible scars on the mirrors of the restaurant. This clearly, and almost painfully, expresses the transient and adaptable nature of the location.

Architects | unit-berlin
Project address | Karl-Liebknecht-Straße 9, 10178 Berlin, Germany
Original use | hungarian cultural institute
Completion of existing building | 1968
Function today | restaurant, bar, cultural events, exhibitions
Completion of conversion | 2010

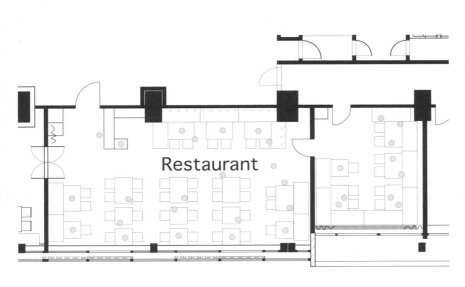

Restaurant

BARBICAN FOODHALL AND LOUNGE

Two new dining destinations enhance one of London's most iconic architectural landmarks, matching the center's reputation for excellence in the arts.

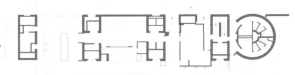

Architects | SHH
Project address | The Barbican Centre, Silk Street, London, UK
Original use | cafe and restaurant
Completion of existing building | 1982
Function today | foodhall and bar/restaurant
Completion of conversion | 2010

Barbican Foodhall is a restaurant and shop with a range of deli products to buy or consume. The design approach linked the space to the architecture of the Barbican and celebrated the building's materiality by exposing the original concrete ceilings and using Cradley brick pavers to match the existing external walkways. Barbican Lounge is a 150-cover restaurant on the first floor. The Lounge has material links to its ground floor sister space, but also boasts a very individual and bold design treatment in striking colors. Design features include a striking 14-meter black mosaic bar, which continues through the glazing onto the outside terrace and a peacock-green resin floor especially color-matched to a photo taken in the summer of the green water of the Barbican outdoor lake.

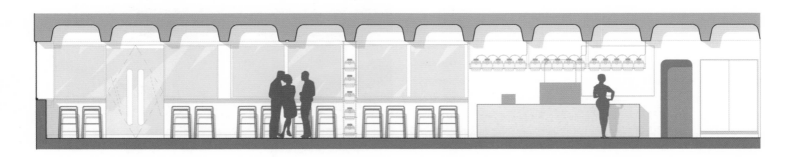

Cahier d'Exercises is located at the entrance level of the historic Donald-Ross II warehouse-store. The limestone façade, cast iron columns, and an expansive brick wall that runs the length of the store recall the 19th century building's industrial past as a retailer of large fabrics, leathers, and furs. A veritable cabinet of curiosities, the seemingly out-of-scale shelving evokes notions of femininity and aspects of secrecy and privacy. Large fitting rooms are hidden from view, and accessed by secret doors in the sculptural shelving system, which displays jewelry, footwear, and accessories. Details like the oval cross section of the racking also add a touch the feminine, as do dabs of phosphorescent vermillion red amid the store's mostly black and white color palette. At the store's entrance, the herringbone-patterned steel floor — a signature of the space — invites visitors to relax in the warmth and comfort of the fireplace.

96

CAHIER D'EXERCICES

Explore a new meaning of black-and-white thinking!

Architects | SAUCIER + PERROTTE ARCHITECTES
Project address | Montréal, Québec, Canada
Original use | warehouse store
Completion of existing building | 1860
Function today | women's boutique
Completion of conversion | 2011

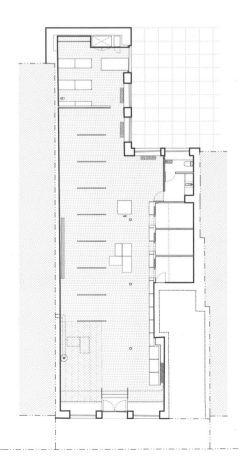

MANOR HOUSE STABLES

Living like a champ! Once retirement home of the glorious racehorse "Lovely Cottage", now a sophisti-cated contemporary family residence.

The concept for this piece of historical heritage was to preserve the existing while making any new additions simple to let the original character shine. The Stables benefits from three double bedrooms with two en suite rooms to accompany a spacious bathroom. Being a single story property with continuous views, the layout was split between sleeping and living accommodations with a single constant circulation running through the entire building. The spacious open-plan kitchen and dining area is located at the heart of the home leading into the roomy lounge, which benefits from full height glazed doors that open out onto the village setting.

Architects | AR DESIGN STUDIO LTD
Project address | Winchester, Hampshire, UK
Original use | stables
Completion of existing building | 18th century
Function today | residential building
Completion of conversion | 2013

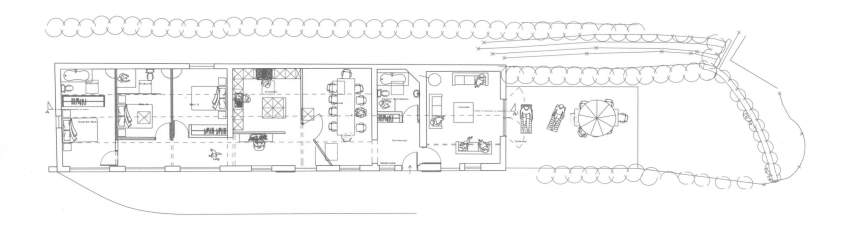

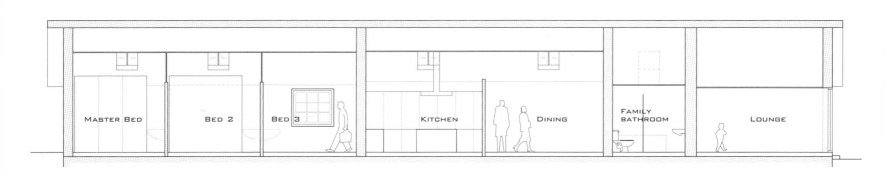

MASTER BED   BED 2   BED 3   KITCHEN   DINING   FAMILY BATHROOM   LOUNGE

OTHER MUSIC ACADEMY

Tell me a story – Minimal interventions preserve and support the ancient charm!

Architects | StudioCE Architects Christian Dengler Holger Schwarz
Project address | Ernst-Kohl-Straße 23, 99423 Weimar, Germany
Original use | customs house, land registry office, primary school
Completion of existing building | 1908
Function today | Other Music Academy, performing arts center
Completion of conversion | 2012

The design idea reflects the values of diversity and sustainability by framing the existing spatial and structural elements of the old building. Infrastructural and technical renovations are restricted to minimal interventions. The basic design principle is a visual representation of point and line. Mostly new surface-mounted elements incorporate the required modernized technical infrastructures, which allow the rich textures and layers of the building's history to remain and to tell its own story. The original parts and textures are framed by the linear elements of the new infrastructures wherever possible. All interventions are made of wood and partly combined with recycled building materials. New timber elements are painted grey to juxtapose them with the recycled materials.

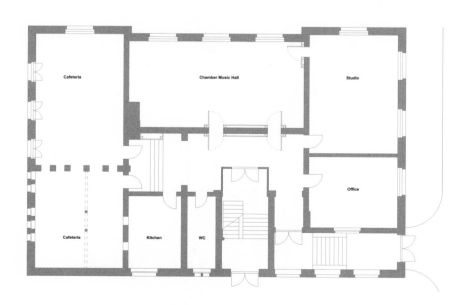

USED

UNIQUE

UNASSUMING

ROUGH

interiors

UNORTHODOX

UNPARALLELED

USEFUL

UPGRADING

NOMA LAB

The creative summit of Danish gastronomy
and architecture.

Architects | GXN - The Innovation Unit of 3XN Architects
Project address | Strandgade 93, Copenhagen, Denmark
Original use | storage building
Completion of existing building | unknown
Function today | restaurant
Completion of conversion | 2012

The NOMA Lab is connected to NOMA situated in a former warehouse on the national registry of protected buildings. The tight restrictions meant that GXN was required to design the interior without using so much as one single nail in the walls or flooring. The approach was to design four central multi-functional storage units; each composed of more than five hundred uniquely formed wooden cubes. Curving playfully throughout the space, these units divide the 200-square-meter space into smaller areas accommodating the food lab, the herbal garden, staff areas, and offices. Raw and simple in color and shape, it captures a unique Nordic aesthetic. True to the restaurant's philosophy, the NOMA Lab is developed using Nordic materials exclusively.

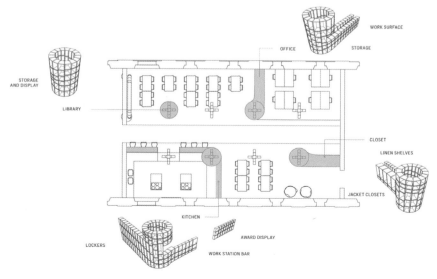

STORAGE AND DISPLAY

LIBRARY

LOCKERS

KITCHEN

WORK STATION BAR

AWARD DISPLAY

OFFICE

WORK SURFACE

STORAGE

CLOSET

LINEN SHELVES

JACKET CLOSETS

For the "12th plan-project" in Cologne, this room in a hall of the DQE was designed for lectures and workshops. The freely suspended wooden laths and fluorescent lamps combine into a translucent curtain floating above the white rectangular carpet. The roughly cut wood, white carpet, and clear neon light contrast with the existing structure and the traces of the automotive workshop, creating a new layer for the theme of the architecture biennale exhibition "Scenario of a city worth living in".

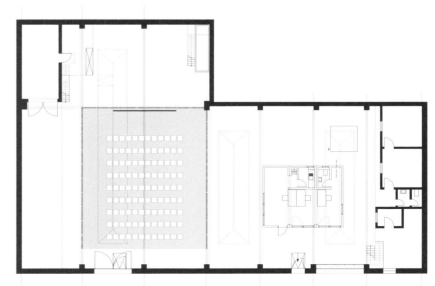

CURTAIN

A light gust of wind and the suspended wooden laths of the curtain twist around their own axes, as everything begins to shimmer.

Architects | LHVH ARCHITEKTEN
Project address | DQE (design quartier ehrenfeld), Heliosstraße 35–37, 50825 Cologne, Germany
Original use | garage
Completion of existing building | 1865
Function today | exhibition, gallery
Completion of conversion | 2011

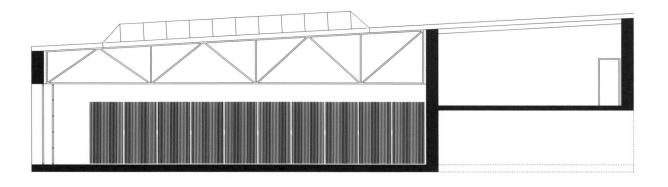

FRANKFURT HISTORICAL MUSEUM

Stone witnesses to history become exhibition
objects themselves, telling their centuries-old story.

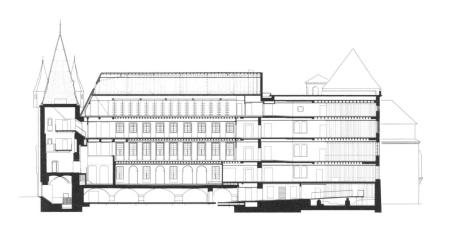

Architects | Diezinger Architekten GmbH (formerly Diezinger & Kramer)
Project address | Fahrtor 2, 60311 Frankfurt, Germany
Original use | medieval fortress, fortified tower, residential building, customs house
Completion of existing building | 12th–19th century
Function today | historical museum
Completion of conversion | 2012

At the heart of Frankfurt's historic quarters, the old city fortifications are the foundation for the old buildings of the Frankfurt historical museum – including Frankfurt's oldest standing building. Undergoing work from the 12th to the 19th century, the interior of the complex, which consists of five different buildings, was changed beyond recognition. The substance and the concept of the complex were basically reconstructed and brought to the technical level of modern museums. The existing historic elements were preserved and new elements added. The renovation strengthened the complex as an entity, while restoring the unique identity of the different building sections with their typical exterior and interior design styles.

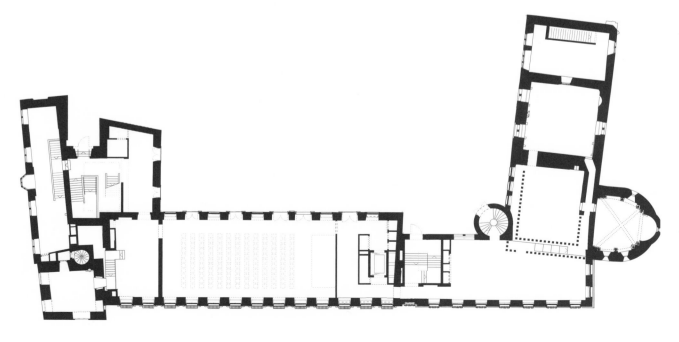

SURGERY DR. B

Tough shell, soft interior – an unconventional
clinic landscape.

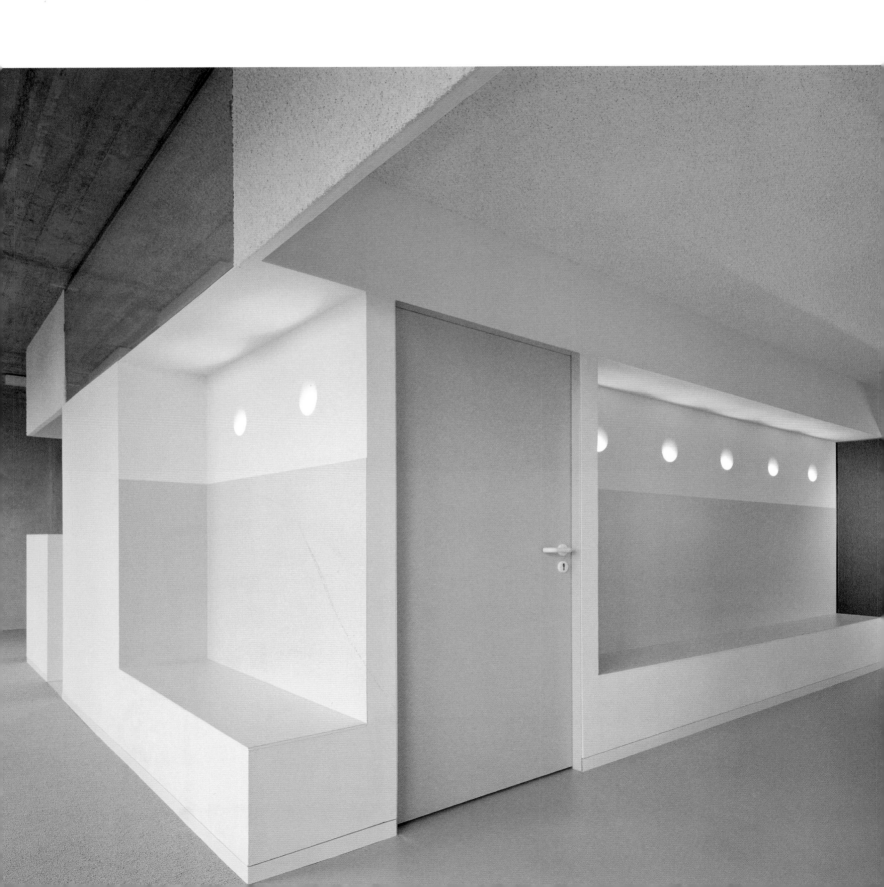

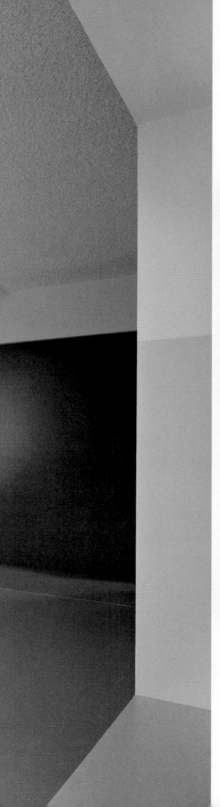

With the aim of maintaining the greatest possible ceiling height to create generously proportioned spaces, the doctor's surgery was not fitted with suspended ceilings and the concrete walls were left unfinished. The rough, unadorned charm of the surrounding waiting areas now contrasts sharply with the careful and finely structured design of the treatment rooms at the core of the clinic. A resourceful mix of various materials such as structured sound-absorbing plaster, glass, and colored sections results in intimate comfortable rooms. If required, drop sides and sliding walls allow the division of the clinic into up to three separately accessible units. The material mix of the unconventional clinic landscape is a refreshing alternative to the high-gloss esthetics of conventional clinics.

Architects | AMUNT - Architekten Martenson und Nagel Theissen
Project address | Volmarstraße 16, 70794 Filderstadt, Bernhausen, Germany
Original use | office building
Completion of existing building | 2010
Function today | surgery
Completion of conversion | 2011

125

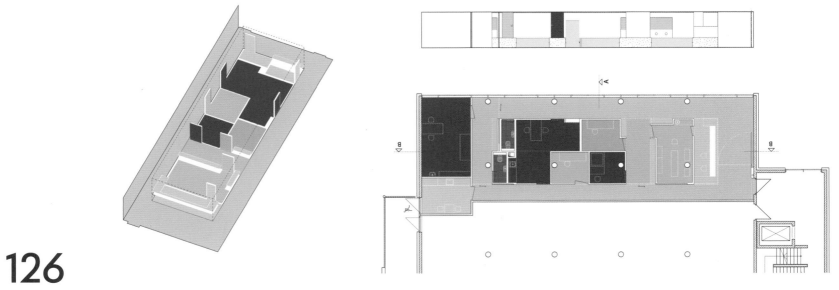

126

HÖST RESTAURANT

Höst and New Norm Dinnerware – a symbiotic
relationship of contrasts.

Architects | Norm Architects X Menu
Project address | Nørre Farimagsgade 41, 1364 Copenhagen, Denmark
Original use | unknown
Completion of existing building | unknown
Function today | restaurant
Completion of conversion | 2012

Norm Architects and Danish design house Menu have joined forces with Copenhagen restaurateurs Cofoco, to create a distinctly urban restaurant with obvious romantic and rural references. Höst is an embodiment of the clash between romanticism and modernity. It is a space of multiple stories that intertwine and correlate to create an inspirational and aesthetic universe for all the senses. An obvious and reoccurring characteristic of both concept and cooperation is the juxtaposition of elements. Höst is rustic gone simplistic. Rural gone urban. Past gone contemporary. The classic virtues of Nordic cooking have found their contemporary expression at Höst.

129

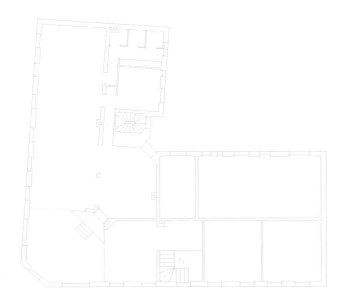
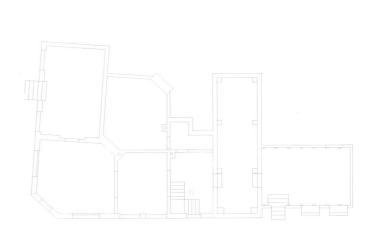

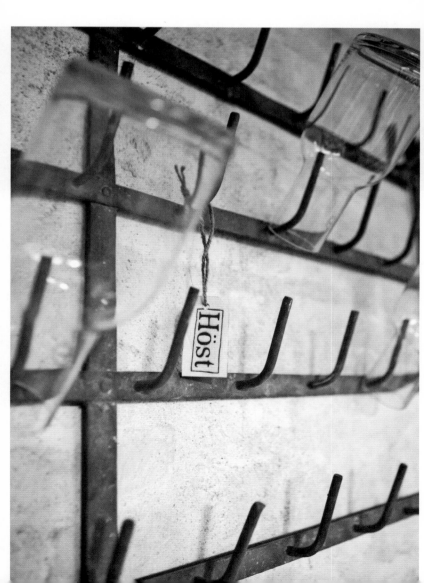

131

A uniform cladding wraps the whole farm. The challenge of the project was to preserve its appearance while filtering light into the heart of the building. The traditional technique of decorative wood cutouts was used to create specific perforations within the planks. The pattern within the cladding was designed to match the path described by the shadows on the façade. Based on this, the project was called the "solar house" – a house exposed on its four façades to the path of the sun and perceived as a sundial. The restoration was based on the key aim of conserving the overall appearance of the existing interior structure. To clear the room of the nave while maintaining the needs of a rental house, the utility functions were closely integrated into the four angular volumes.

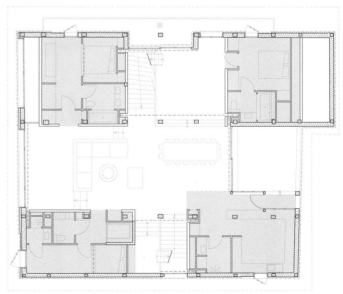

VILLA SOLAIRE

Reach for the sun and enjoy your stay in this luxury rental villa.

Architects and interior designers | JKA - Jérémie Koempgen Architecture / FUGA - J. Aich & M. Recordon designers
Project address | Chemin du pied de la Plagne, Morzine, France
Original use | farmhouse
Completion of existing building | 1826
Function today | rental house
Completion of conversion | 2012

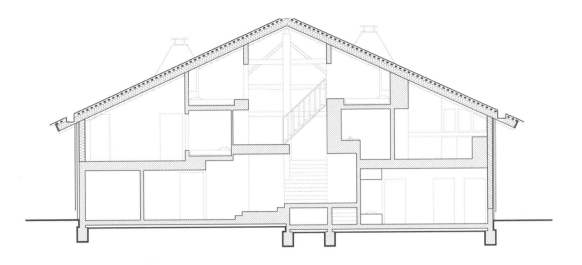

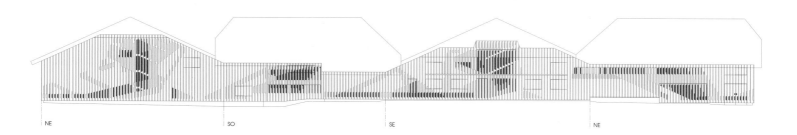

NE   SO   SE   NE

The Botín Foundation chose a 1920s Silversmith workshop to establish its new offices in Madrid. The principal objective of the architectural concept was to once again allow natural light to permeate the entire building. Not only were the filled-in windows and skylights reopened, but the internal layout was also altered to create a double-height atrium for use as the main lobby. The direct daylight and natural vegetation give character and personality to this meeting place. The project aims to reveal the historical changes of the building by exposing the original steel and brickwork; the various alterations of the past; and by contrast, the new construction work whose finishes mainly consist of oak, steel and glass.

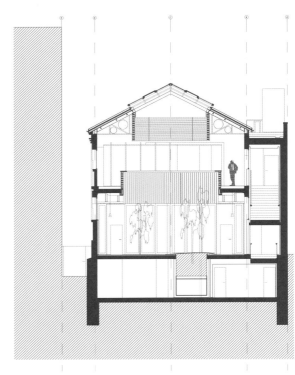

136

BOTÍN FOUNDATION

Retaining the spirit of the original industrial
character, MVN Arquitectos created spacious,
light-flooded and modern office space.

Architects | Diego Varela de Ugarte and Emilio Medina Garcia, MVN architects
Interior Designer | Juan Luis Líbano
Project address | Madrid, Spain
Original use | Vinçon shop, Silversmith workshop
Completion of existing building | 1920
Function today | office building
Completion of conversion | 2012

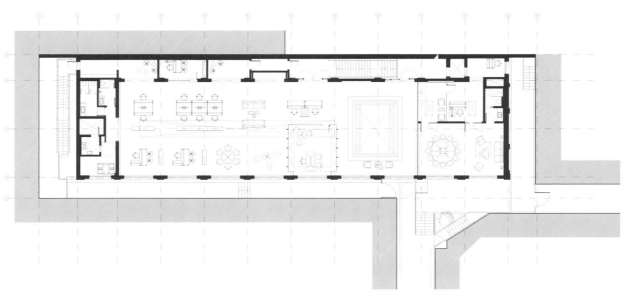

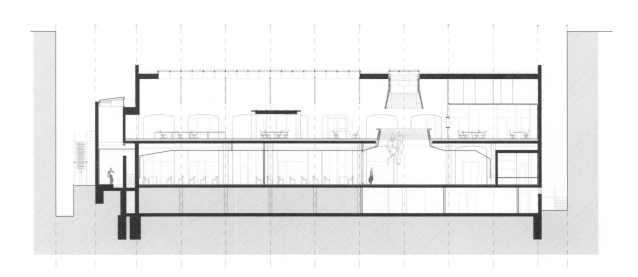

BULLEREI RESTAURANT

From livestock transport to trendy gourmet eatery.
A very special visit to a restaurant radiating
industrial charm and classical design.

Architects | Giorgio Gullotta Architekten
Accessoires | Kathrin Bade
Project address | Lagerstraße 34 B, 20357 Hamburg,
Germany
Original use | meat market
Completion of existing building | unknown
Function today | restaurant
Completion of conversion | 2009

The Bullerei is located in the revamped and modernized livestock halls of the former wholesale meat market. The restaurant as well as the deli and day bar are in the entry way and in parts of the West Hall. The various areas are connected by a kitchen which is the heart of the ensemble. It opens to the dining rooms via a glazed window and integrated display case. The hall character is retained by the arrangement of the individual functional areas. Tumbled bluestone was used for floor material, while the walls are partially unplastered. The dining tables made of 300 year old oak are framed with modern graffiti, interspersed with high-gloss tables and chairs made of scraps of wood. It is the interaction between historical structure and modern architecture which lends the restaurant its atmosphere.

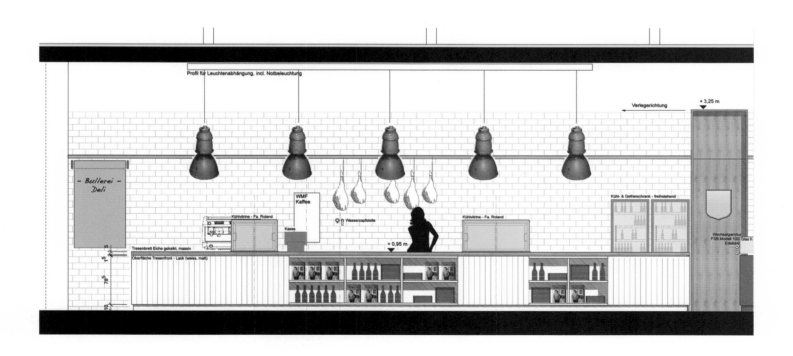

Layers of time expressed in space. When building director Ott began construction of the building in 1732, he could not envision the changes the building would undergo one day. Just about 130 years later, it was turned into a royal court library and another 140 years later, in 2011, the building took on a new series of functions. This time it became the home of an events venue, a restaurant, and a museum. What would the venerable Mr. Ott say if he could visit his building 280 years after it was built? He would probably marvel at the many changes and admire the used materials such as Corten steel and concrete. At any rate, he would certainly appreciate the fact that great care and diligence were applied to maintaining his building for the future.

OLD COURT LIBRARY

As time goes by... From a chancellery to a court library to a restaurant and museum – what's next?

Architects | gäbele & raufer . architekten . BDA
Project address | Haldenstraße 5, 78166 Donaueschingen, Germany
Original use | chancellery, court library
Completion of existing building | 1732
Function today | restaurant, function rooms, museum
Completion of conversion | 2011

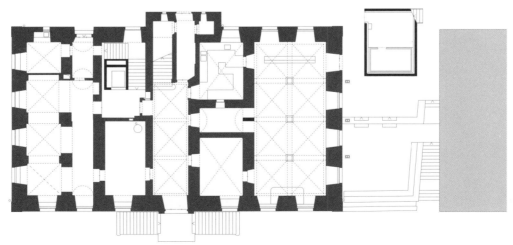

HORIZONTAL SHOWCASE

The beauty and the beast: The raw, unrefined space provides the backdrop to showcase a collection of highly sophisticated garments.

Architects | Serrano + Baquero Arquitectos
Project address | Calle Puerta Real N°1,
Arcade Local 2, 18009 Granada, Spain
Original use | fragrance store
Completion of existing building | unknown
Function today | clothing store
Completion of conversion | 2010

Serrano + Baquero Arquitectos were commissioned to transform a former fragrance store in a shopping arcade in the center of Granada into a clothing store. The unattractive location and poorly lit interior overwhelmed with windows and shutters presented a host of obstacles that demanded careful consideration. The result is a compelling space in which private and public areas become blurred and indistinct and where the essential elements are discovered: exposed cement walls, a brick vault, the concrete ceiling structure and moldings. Choosing to radically strip the existing architecture of all that was unnecessary, the designers opened the door to a new type of fashion store.

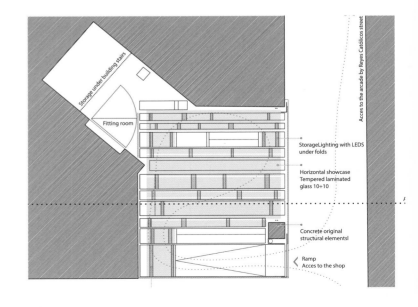

FRESH RESTAURANT

Russia's capital goes green. The Sundukovy Sisters
mix history and contemporary design for an
eclectic eatery.

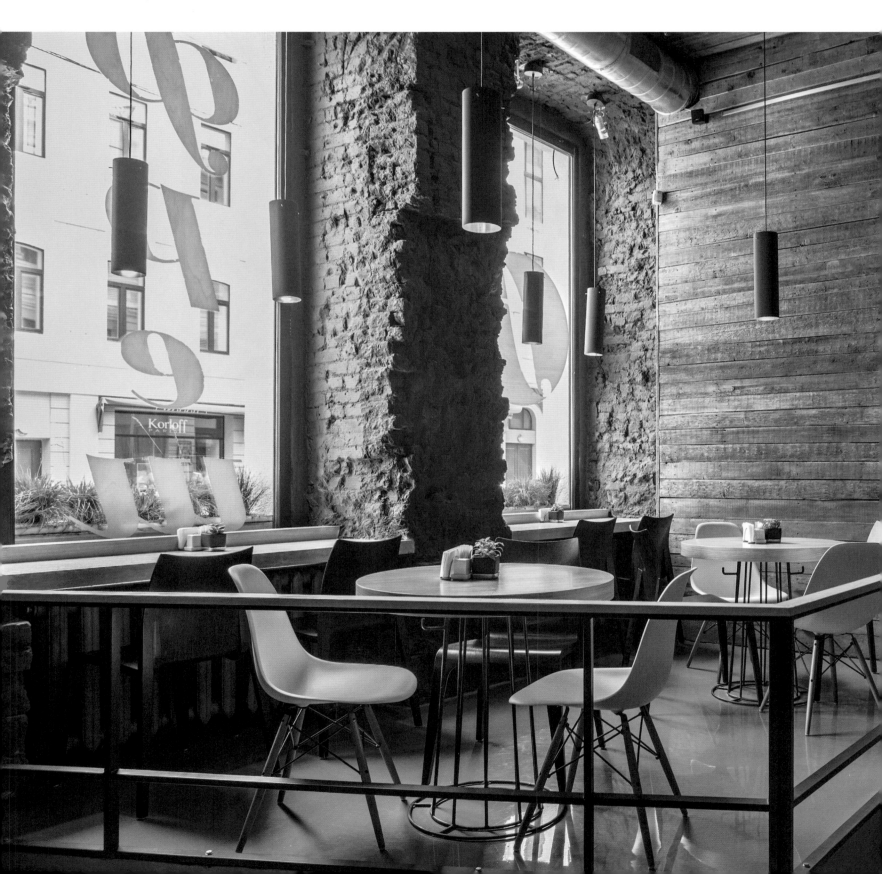

In August 2012, vegetarian restaurant Fresh was opened in Moscow, promoting the idea of cool and diverse healthy nutrition and lifestyle. The minimalistic interior combines brickwork of the 19th century with modern concrete. Old boards from Russian villages cover the walls and ceiling, partially painted in green. The furniture is simple, yet functional – a smart mix of Eames' style icons, rather simple chairs made of plywood and tables designed by the Sundukovy Sisters. The interior is as simple and honest, yet contemporary and stylish as Fresh's healthy and honest food.

Architects | Sundukovy Sisters Studio
Project address | Moscow, Russia
Original use | unknown
Completion of existing building | 1917
Function today | restaurant
Completion of conversion | 2012

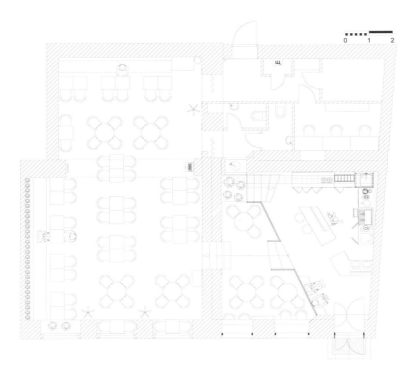

157

GREAT

GNARLY

GENUINE

ROUGH

interiors

GRITTY

GRUFF

GALLIONIC

GLAUCOUS

JAFFA\TEL AVIV

Mix it up! The restaurant as a melting pot
of culinary excellence and design.

Architects | Baranowitz & Kronenberg Architecture Studio
Project address | 98 Yigal Alon Street, Tel Aviv, Israel
Function | restaurant
Completion | 2011

BK's basic aim was to represent the spirit of Cohen Kitchen – a genuine yet
sophisticated blend of culinary traditions. The restaurant is enveloped in very basic
materials: water, cement, and steel. Exactly like Haim's cuisine consisting of water,
flour and olive oil. Like the ingredients, which come from different countries, many
different design elements are mixed together. They evoke also the flair of old Jaffa,
a city where multi-national traditions live side by side. The mix of different elements
represents a cultural melting pot. The space is divided into three areas: the poured
terrazzo bar, the dining hall, and the open kitchen where guests are invited to sit
around the fire and enjoy the chef's crew show. The kitchen's stainless steel tops
become a huge dining countertop.

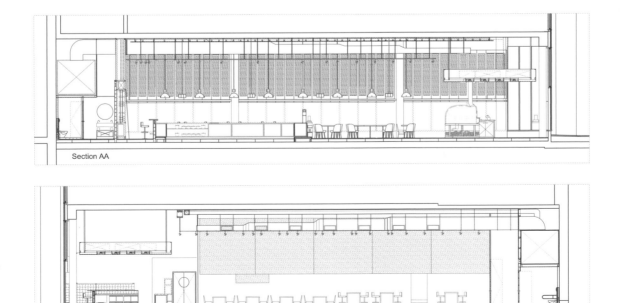

Section AA

Section BB

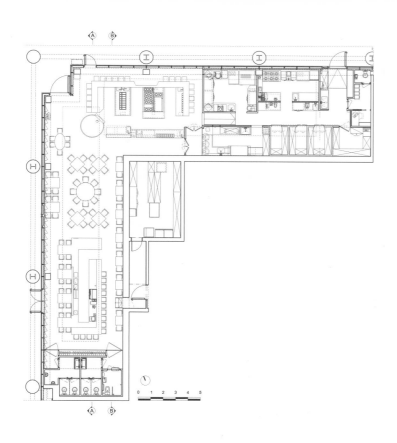

HOTEL SCHOLL

A house built in 1492 makes the leap into the 21st century – contemporary design combined with a late medieval half-timbered façade.

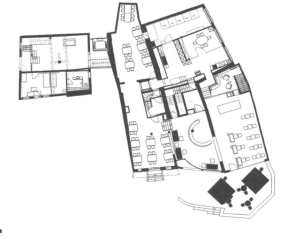

164

Architects and interior designer | seifried&mack interior design / METZGER+HULSMANN
Project address | Klosterstraße 2–4, 74523 Schwäbisch-Hall, Germany
Original use | hotel, residence
Completion of existing building | 1492
Function today | hotel
Completion of conversion | 2012

In the conversion of Hotel Scholl in Schwäbisch Hall, Germany, the two interior designers seifried&mack applied their principle of creating rooms that awaken interest, impress with their powerful visual concept, yet are functional at the same time. The result is unique contemporary design in the middle of a late medieval half-timbered façade. The guests of the Scholl family can now embark on a journey of discovery through the historic building, where they can find among many other details, a golden curtain made of thousands of aluminum chains, several hundred steel sheet birds, as well as a giant footprint made of Styrofoam that is reminiscent of a former history-charged resident.

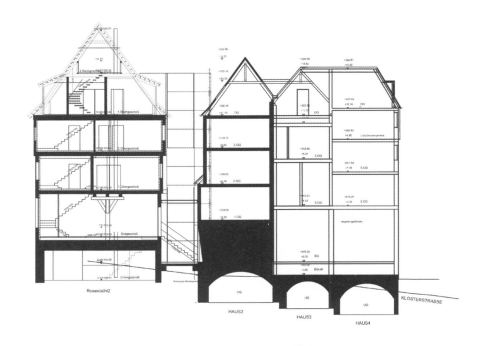

APPARTAMENTO AL

Perfect imperfection. Natural and artificial, contemporary and ancient. All elements form a harmonious whole.

Architects | ARCHIPLANSTUDIO
Project address | Via Bronzetti, 46100 Mantova, Italy
Original use | residential building
Completion of existing building | 1700
Function today | residential building
Completion of conversion | 2011

The domestic dimension of the design is based on a simple and spiritual connotation obtained from the relationships between individual elements that make up the project. The project investigates issues related to the imperfection and the sensuality stemming from the contradiction between the precision and the control of the design and a dimension generated by the passing of time. The result is a set of fuzzy relations between natural and artificial elements. The kitchen was designed by Key and made of concrete on location; the hanging brass furniture was developed by Ghiroldi; the bed, sink and lamps were designed by archiplanstudio; the table and the chairs came from Ikea , while the bathroom mirrors were made by Agape.

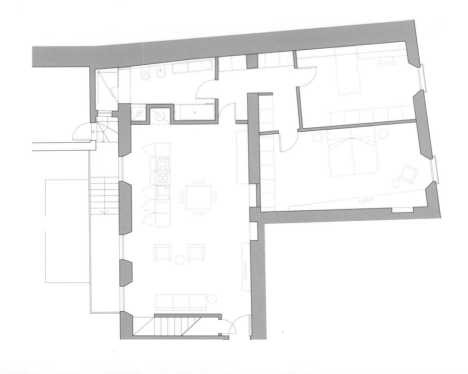

TERRA MINERALIA

Collecting and identifying. A multi-faceted design
for the multi-faceted world of minerals.

Architects | AFF Architekten
Project address | Schlossplatz 4, 09599 Freiberg, Germany
Original use | castle
Completion of existing building | 1577 / 1784
Function today | museum
Completion of conversion | 2008

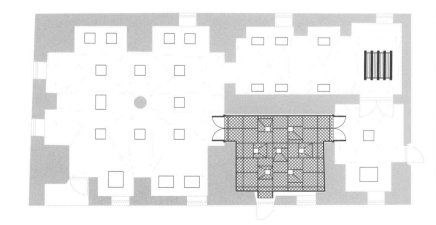

The primary aim was to mediate between the witnesses of the different architectural eras and the various users. A pillar of the success of providing a "forgotten" castle with a face once again was the open collaboration with the department of monument preservation. The project was accompanied by open discussions in which a balance between the preservation of historical structures and the birth of new spatial qualities was sought. After establishing defining basic concepts, such as reestablishing the renaissance design of two building wings, the maintenance of the façades of the Lange Haus and the church wing, and the reconstruction of Saxony's first 16th century parallel staircase, the design focused on the new additions.

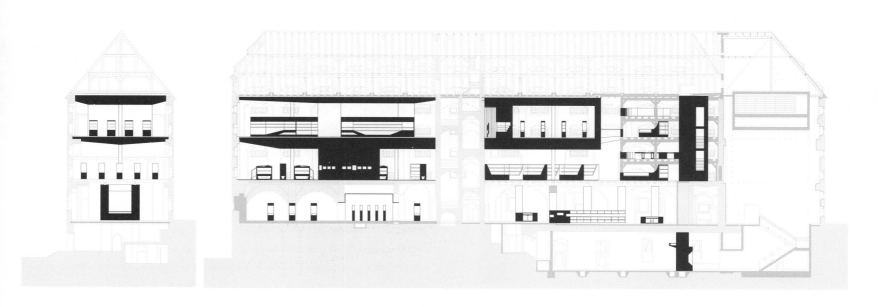

SALON 55

Meet Alice in the wonderland of SALON 55!

Architects | PURPUR Architektur ZT GmbH
Project address | Gumpendorfer Straße 55, 1060 Wien, Austria
Original use | carpet dealer
Completion of existing building | 1880
Function today | SALON 55 – film, art, communication and architecture
Completion of conversion | 2009

Modest, confining, and labyrinthine rooms constituted the premises of the carpet dealer at Gumpendorfer Straße 55. The intention, or rather intuition, to turn them into a PURPUResque studio ambience was implemented by the simplest form of architectural intervention – create a blank slate and see what comes up. For PURPUR, surprising underlying structures came up – the patio, and the 7.5th floor. Carefully and with limited and sometimes improvised selections of materials and interventions they proceeded to keep everything in place while creating a multitude of perspectives, somehow like Alice's rabbit hole – the wonderland of SALON 55.

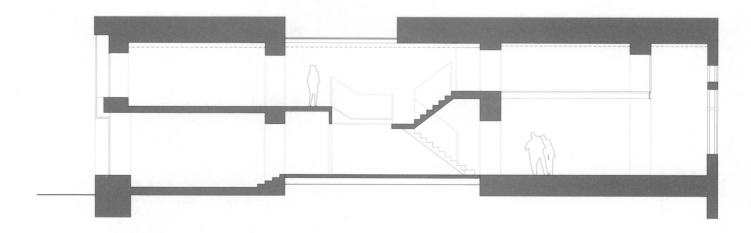

179

SOHO HOUSE

A blend of old Berlin, 1930s and 1940s glamour,
and industrial style. For members only!

Soho House Berlin was developed across eight floors within the historic and imposing Torstraße building. Originally built in 1928, the property, now filled with black and white tiled flooring throughout, oversized seating and fireplaces, will include a members' club, with its own club floor and roof top, and a heated swimming pool, with stunning panoramic views of the Mitte district. The interior design of the space is a collaboration between Soho House in-house designer Susie Atkinson and new commissioner Michaelis Boyd Associates. Together they have delivered a blend of old Berlin, as well as 1930s and 1940s glamour mixed with an eclectic industrial style. Exposed concrete beams and traditional paneling help create a retro industrial feel that echoes Berlin's trademark architectural style.

Architects | Susie Atkinson and Michaelis Boyd Associates
Project address | Torstraße 1, 10178 Berlin, Germany
Original use | unknown
Completion of existing building | 1928
Function today | private members club and hotel
Completion of conversion | 2010

THE SHED

Challenging the notion that bigger is better while exploring the opportunities of adaptive reuse.

Architects | Richard Peters Associates
Project address | Sydney, Australia
Original use | farriers' workshop
Completion of existing building | 1890
Function today | residential building
Completion of conversion | 2010

184

Built in 1890, this former industrial building served as a workshop, warehouse, and artists' studio. Demonstrating the resilience of its heritage fabric, the building is now a house designed with an eye for detail and studied restraint. A series of spaces required for contemporary living were carefully inserted into the simple brick shed in response to the building's long northern elevation, double-height volume, lane access, and views over established gardens. Designer Richard Peters made the most of these qualities in form, material and arrangement, taking cues from the original building and reinforcing the opportunities of adaptive reuse. With a simple palette that employs materials as both structure and finish, The Shed reflects an inquisitive approach to the making of architecture.

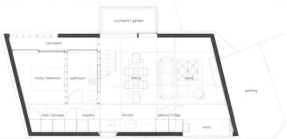

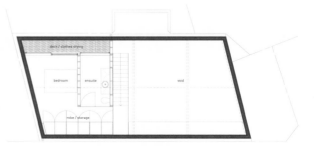

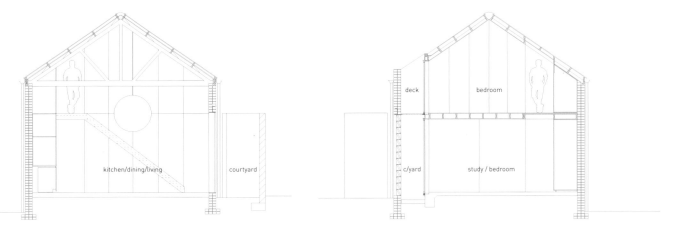

kitchen/dining/living   courtyard

deck   bedroom

c/yard   study / bedroom

186

END...LINK / BEAUTY SALON

A multifunctional wooden framework invites staff and customers to get creative in this Osaka beauty salon.

Architects | Yasunari Tsukada Design
Project address | Kitahorie Nishi-ku Osaka, Japan
Original use | warehouse
Completion of existing building | 1979
Function today | beauty salon
Completion of conversion | 2012

The owner chose a slender, elongated space measuring 28 meters in depth, with a front of just 4.4 meters as the new platform for his venture. Taking advantage of this narrow front, the designer configured each of the spaces in a straightforward manner by taking cues from the existing frame and contours of the property. Painting the entire space white achieved a feeling of abstraction, and gives equal importance to both the new and old materials that comprise the walls, ceilings, and floors. For storing or hanging objects, Tsukada developed a three-dimensional lattice screen resembling parts of a jungle gym that function as architectural pieces of furniture. When lighting fixtures, glass panels, hooks and other objects are attached, the lattice begins to take on a new dimension, turning into display shelves or tables.

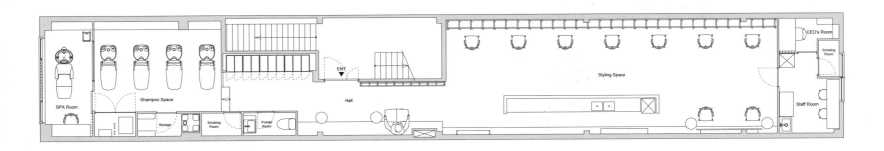

STEAM BLOWER HOUSE

Walls that tell of many years of industrial use today serve as a rehearsal location for musicians and dancers.

Architects | Heinrich Böll Architekt BDA DWB
Client | Nrw. Urban GmbH, Dortmund
Project address | An der Jahrhunderthalle 1, 44793 Bochum, Germany
Original use | steam blower house
Completion of existing building | 1876
Function today | rehearsal stage, technical journal
Completion of conversion | 2011

The steam blower hall of a former steel mill is located in the immediate vicinity of the Jahrhunderthalle, the central venue of the Ruhrtriennale, the annual regional music and arts festival. The listed building was fitted with two rehearsal rooms as well as storage areas for the stage equipment. Its structure consisted primarily of solid reinforced masonry walls that enclosed a narrow and high space from three sides covered with a timber roof. This is topped to this day by an elevated water tank. The reutilization concept added new ceilings in such a way that the required useful spaces were created and the original room height was kept intact in some parts. A new access tower was added on the outside, while the walls remained almost untouched to tell of many years of industrial use.

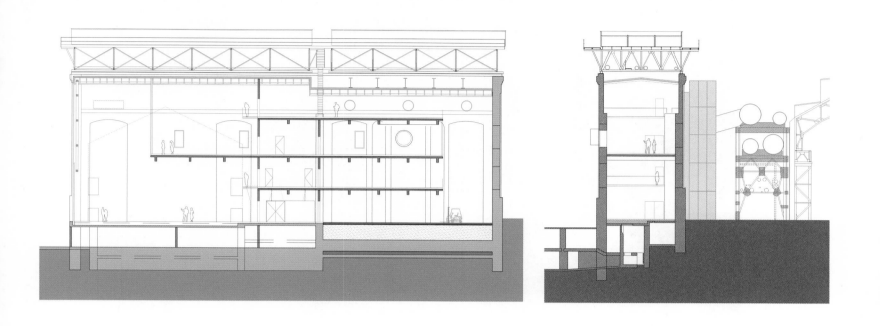

The conversion project of the 16th century tower, a former granary for the Château d'Echandens, aimed to make additional space available in the attic, which was originally only 1.60-meter high. Lowering the suspended ceiling created another 30 square meters of living space. The inserted "parasite" is both autonomous and inextricably merged with the building, as it "inhabits" the entire gutted interior of the original stone structure, completely filling it from the entrance threshold to the new room beneath the rooftop. The intervention plays with the stone material of the existing shell and counteracts it with larch triple-plywood, the material used for the entire construction. The new intervention's wooden material properties make it visible and give it a temporal marker.

TOUR MOINAT

Like a parasite – A new "piece of furniture"
invades the inside of the tower.

Architects | 2b stratégies urbaines concrètes / S. Bender Dr. ès sc. Arch. epfl bsa - Ph. Béboux Arch. epfl sia bsa
Project address | Rue du Château 14,1026 Echandens, Switzerland
Original use | granary
Completion of existing building | 16th century
Function today | residential building
Completion of conversion | 2010

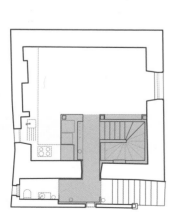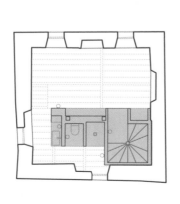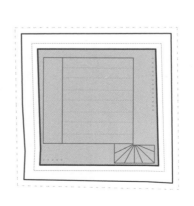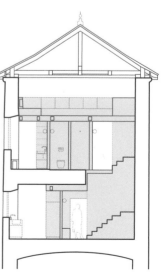

RISTORANTE LACUCINA

Understated elegance. The restaurant in the heart of historic Mantua has an invitingly cozy atmosphere.

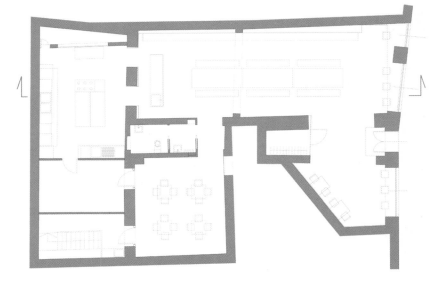

Architects | ARCHIPLANSTUDIO
Project address | Via Oberdan, 46100 Mantova, Italy
Original use | shop
Completion of existing building | 1700
Function today | restaurant
Completion of conversion | 2011

The project aimed to establish relationships between two worlds – old and new, in a balance that maintains the identity of both. Similarly, light and shadow are kept in their ambiguity and plurality, without sacrificing one for the other. The precision of the design is juxtaposed to the imperfection of the existing elements, whose materials exhibit an exceptional energy gained from the passing of time. This relationship was at the core of the design process, focusing on the way in which things are related to generate new knowledge and new beauty. The basic concept was to try to reconcile the opposites, such as the strength and fragility of the perfection and imperfection, the luster of a piece of furniture fresh from the factory with the imperfection of materials fallen into a state of neglect.

203

HIP

HARSH

HISTORICAL

ROUGH
interiors

HARD

HOARY

HAUNTING

GOTTSCHALK'S MILL

Dark red brick stone, light grey exposed concrete, brown timber, glass, and stainless steel – A perfect mix of material and colors.

Architects | Christof Gemeiner Architekten BDA
Project address | Mühle 64, 40724 Hilden, Germany
Original use | granary
Completion of existing building | 1846
Function today | events venue
Completion of conversion | 2012

The granary, which serves as an events venue today, was in a derelict state before its renovation. Therefore, the open gallery level made of exposed concrete was added to reinforce the building structure. The old roof truss with the prominent strutted frame had to be replaced by a new one and therefore no longer serves a function, but was kept in the space. The masonry was only cleaned to allow all traces of the former use to remain visible. An old miller's trick was used for fitting the original stairway of the mill building – it was mounted back to front so that the worn steps are now situated in the back and in the front there are "new" straight stairs that can comfortably be used again.

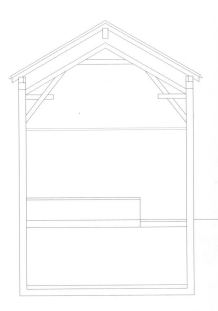

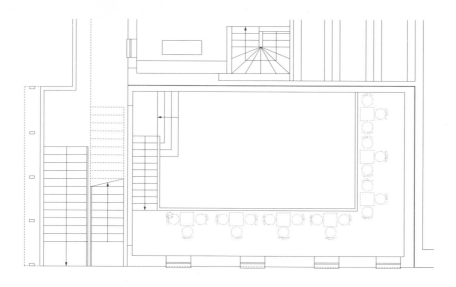

ANCIENT GRANGE

Big is beautiful. Extraordinary living in an old granary.

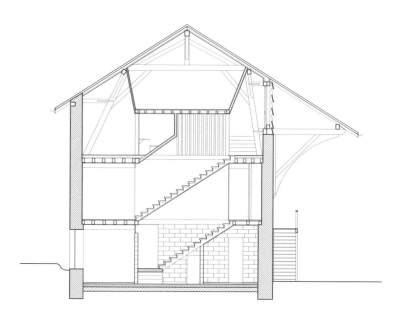

Architects | Charles Pictet Architecte FAS SIA
Project address | Landecy, GE, Switzerland
Original use | grange
Completion of existing building | 19th century
Function today | residential building
Completion of conversion | 2012

The estate of Landecy was created over several centuries and has always been owned by the same family. The farmhouse became an elegant residence in the eighteenth century, surrounded by a dozen buildings enclosed in courtyards and gardens. The latest building of this estate is a granary dating from the second half of the nineteenth century, an impressive building called the "big barn" by the owner family. After being simply empty for over 20 years, it was recently decided to turn the large 19th century barn into a house. The rule of the game was to change the use while preserving everything on the site: the building and its spirit.

213

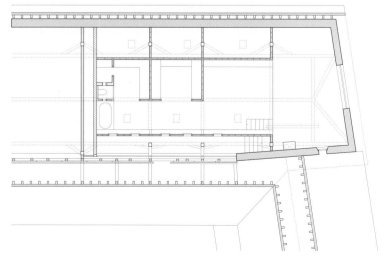

OTTAKRINGER BREWERY

"History flows forward in rivers of beer". Time passes, things change, but the Ottakringer brewery is still up-to-date. Today it's not just a brewery, it's also a place to be.

Architects | Giorgio Gullotta Architekten
Project address | Ottakringer Brauerei AG, Ottakringer Platz 1, 1160 Vienna, Austria
Original use | warehouse; gymnasium; factory
Completion of existing building | 1837
Function today | brewery, event location
Completion of conversion | 2012

Ottakringer is the last of the big Viennese breweries. Established in 1837 it is a family-owned business. The brewery premises contain the production and warehouse areas, the administration as well as the generously sized event area. This consists of a number of different rooms located in the public section of the brewery facing the city. One of these venues is the hop storage room. Before the restructuring, it was dark and gloomy, yet with great potential due to its visible timber beams. A new bar, matching wooden floor and a new illumination concept revived the room. The bar is covered in craquelure tiles that were delivered specifically for the brewery in a golden beer shade.

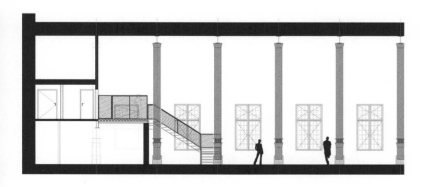

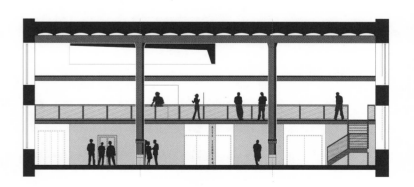

KANTOOR IMD

A playground for engineers! The new IMD headquarters offers an unorthodox working environment.

Architects | Ector Hoogstad Architecten
Project address | 77 Piekstraat, Rotterdam, The Netherlands
Original use | steel plant
Completion of existing building | 1951
Function today | office
Completion of conversion | 2011

The design strategy positioned all work areas on two floors in air-conditioned zones against the closed end walls. From there, they overlook the hall, in which pavilions with conference areas were created, interlinked by footbridges and various types of stairs. An unusual layout for an office building, it allows users to be in constant contact with its spatial and social heart, stimulating interaction. The hall itself was designed as a weakly air-conditioned cavity, which lends itself very well to many uses, including informal consultations, lectures, exhibitions and lunching. Large new windows in what was originally a closed façade, in combination with the existing skylights in the roof, provide daylight and magnificent panoramic views of the water.

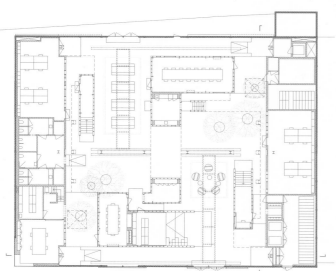

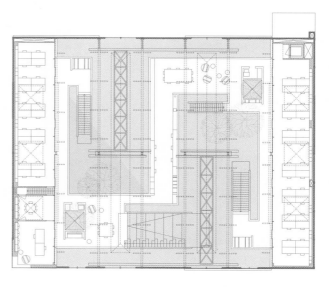

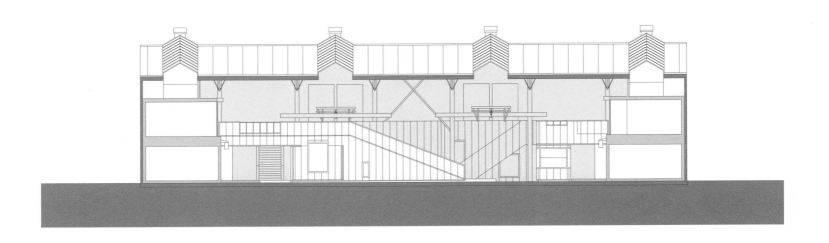

KAISERPFALZ GELNHAUSEN

A symbiosis of historic sandstone and raw steel.

Architects | Pahl + Weber-Pahl Architekten BDA
Project address | Burgstraße 14, 63571 Gelnhausen, Germany
Original use | medieval imperial palace
Completion of existing building | 1200
Function today | museum
Completion of conversion | 2007

The aim was to preserve the historically significant imperial palace of Gelnhausen, dating back to emperor Barbarossa, making it accessible to visitors. Pahl + Weber-Pahl developed a structure of weather-resistant steel and oak that is almost freely floating inside the historic tower fragment. The entire vertical access is suspended from an eight-meter high steel panel. The contrasting and unrelated materials of raw steel to milled sandstone have a formidable attractive effect. The impression is supported on the inside by the daylight that enters freely from an unframed glass roof and staggered oak slats.

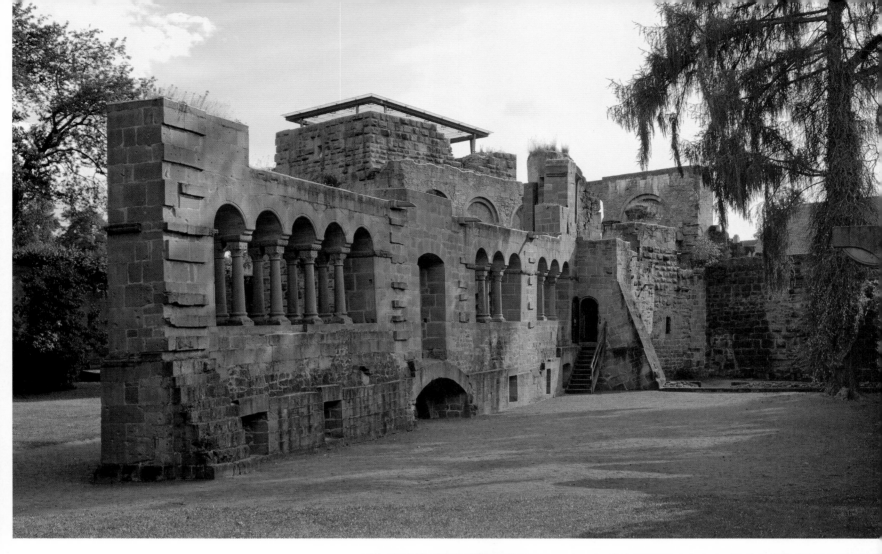

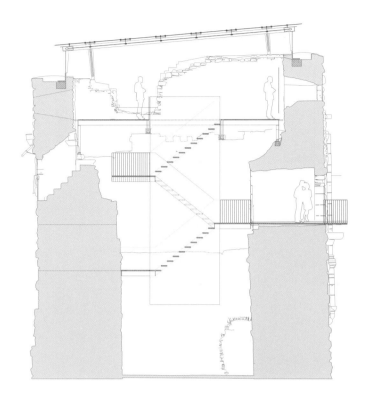

228

CASALE IN CHIANTI

A combination of rural charm, comfort, and technology. This private house is a jewel of gentle renovation.

Architects | Arch. Barbara Monica, Studio Rosso 19
Project address | Chianti, Tuscany, Italy
Original use | private house farm
Completion of existing building | 1980
Function today | private house farm
Completion of conversion | 2012

As the original building was a farm, the project was based on the concept of using natural and simple materials. The living rooms are expansive and open and the big kitchen, separated from them only by a big brickwork oven, is part of the large space and serves as a friendly meeting point. On the same level, there is a guest bedroom and two bathrooms. On the second floor, the sleeping area consists of a master bedroom and two children's rooms. Each room has a private bathroom. Great attention was given to the used materials – kitchen plans and sinks are made of concrete, the kitchen furniture is covered by sheets of aged iron, while the rooms feature traditional lime plaster.

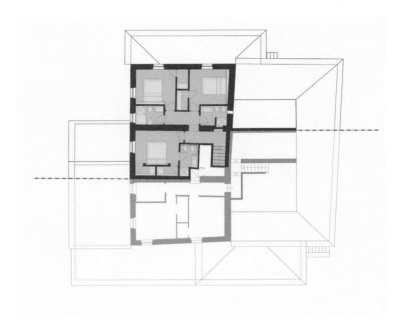

233

TEXTILWERK

Revive and add new life. From a former rope chamber to a human energy transmission room.

Architects | ATELIER BRÜCKNER GmbH
Project address | Industriestraße 5, 46395 Bocholt, Germany
Original use | spinnery
Completion of existing building | 1907, 1950
Function today | cultural center, exhibition, event areas
Completion of conversion | 2011

The TextilWerk Bocholt features a subtle dialog between its historic building substance and contemporary architectural accents. The architectural monument elements with the traces of its former usage and unique aura is sharply interposed to the new structural layer. The targeted respectful interceptions underline the original functional connections within the factory. The shapes and colors are based on the original building. The central rope chamber, previously serving the transmission of power from the steam engines to the weaving rooms, now offers central access to the building. Lightly oscillating flights of stairs were mounted as an interpretation of the former transmission ropes. The newly added top structure serves as a long-distance attraction point with a metaphoric magnetism.

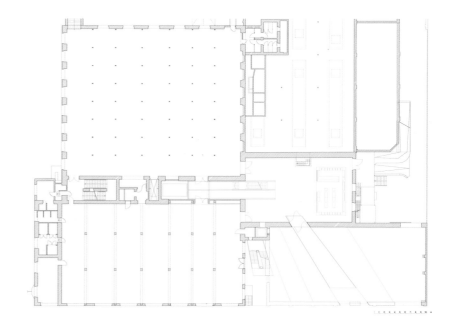

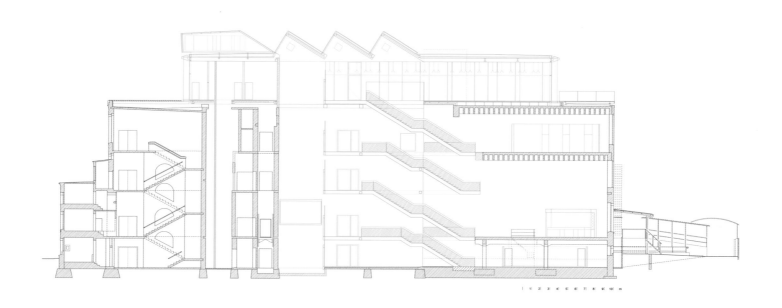

236

25HOURS HOTEL HAFENCITY

A modern maritime story: the hotel is not only the first in Hamburg's new urban district of Hafencity – it is also its new living room.

Architects | Stephen Williams Associates
Project address | Überseeallee 5, 20457 Hamburg, Germany
Function | hotel
Completion | 2011

The hotel offers a classical typology of spaces but comes up with surprising interpretations. The rooms are cabin-style suites, the business center is called the "Radio Room" and the "Hafen Sauna" on the rooftop is built within a rusty container with panoramic view. The ground floor, with lobby, restaurant, bar and shop presents a comfortable version of harbor living and serves as the hub of the hotel. A Hapag-Lloyd shipping container doubles as a conference room. The vinyl library is a great place to socialize and explore. In the rooms, a 'travel trunk' is used as working desk and mini bar. The 25hours Hotel Hafencity is a space of cultural relevance – a place to interact, and a destination that invites you to start exploring it by yourself.

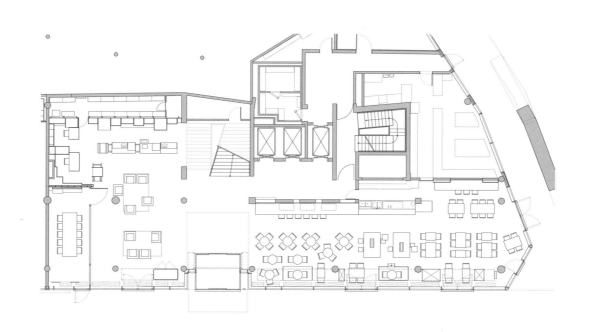

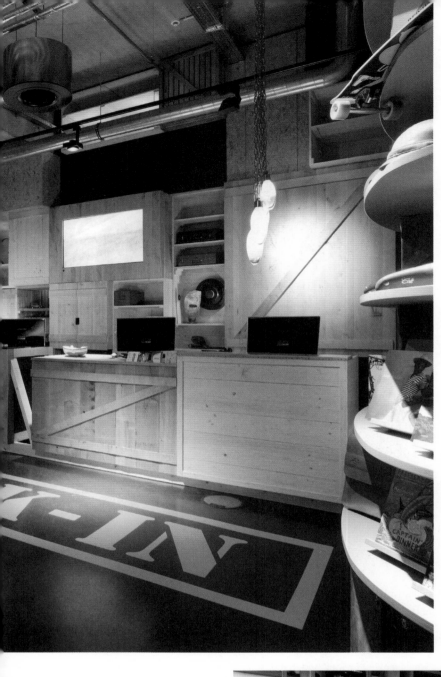

CARICATURA

Confined and spacious, old and new. The implanted exhibition furniture creates a dynamic interplay.

Architects | Diezinger Architekten GmbH (formerly Diezinger & Kramer)
Project address | Weckmarkt 17, 60311 Frankfurt, Germany
Original use | Leinwandhaus, restaurant, photo gallery
Completion of existing building | 14th century
Function today | museum comic art
Completion of conversion | 2008

Built in the 14th century, the unique Leinwandhaus exhibits all the characteristics of secular Geometric style architecture. In 1983 the war-ravaged building was reconstructed with the original exterior. Caricatura, the Museum of Comic Art, aims to provide an appropriate place that honors the caricaturists and authors of the so-called "New Frankfurt School" and that documents and exhibits the various facets of their art form. The construction measures focused mainly only changing the interior room structure. The ground floor is flexibly used for rotating exhibitions and special events. The new gallery, a furniture-like extension, is available as an expanded exhibition space. The second floor houses the permanent exhibition, the third floor and roof floors contain the administration offices.

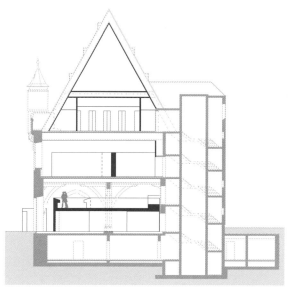

LEISTIKOWSTRASSE 1
MEMORIAL AND MEETING PLACE

"No Design". Not staged and not reconstructed.
The building is the key exhibit of the exhibition.

Architects | GERHARDS&GLÜCKER
Project address | Leistikowstraße 1, 14469 Potsdam, Germany
Original use | rectory, remand prison, warehouse
Completion of existing building | 1916
Function today | memorial and meeting place
Completion of conversion | 2012

The building of the former remand center is the key exhibit of the permanent exhibition. Because the exhibition venue is a former residential building, the design deliberately avoided classical museum elements such as box-shaped stands, pedestals, and display cases to keep the rawness of the site intact. Instead, delicate exhibition furniture items were developed that cover up as little as possible of the original site. The cruel fate of the victims is communicated via a "biography table" that contains personal items, a portrait, and the biography of each victim. Relatives can sit at the table to remember the victim. The illumination concept supports the intimacy of the remembrance process.

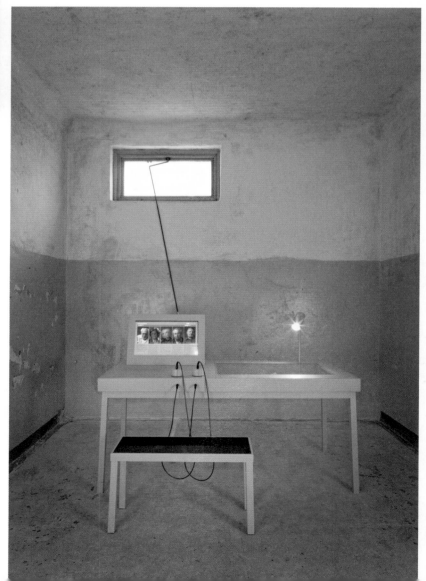

DABBOUS

A raw industrial language is used that juxtaposes award-winning chef Ollie Dabbous's delicate dishes.

Architects | Brinkworth
Project address | 39 Whitfield St, London, W1T 2SF, UK
Original use | unknown
Completion of existing building | unknown
Function today | restaurant and bar
Completion of conversion | 2012

Brinkworth created a sparse and unexpected backdrop for a unique dining experience, using steel, wire mesh, concrete, timber, and reeded glass to define the environment. An eclectic selection of light fixtures and customized furniture softens the otherwise brutal material palette. The site extends across two floors, with access to the raw and minimal bar downstairs through the ground floor restaurant. A custom-made metal mesh structure screens the traffic to the bar from the dining space and doubles up as a coat hanger, while creating an acoustic buffer between the two spaces. The large windows of the corner site flood the restaurant with light in the daytime, while at night the windows reflect the sparkly effect of the interior lighting.

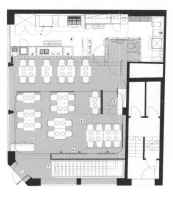
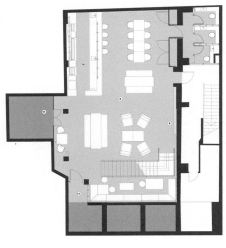

251

INDEX

IMPRINT

The Deutsche Nationalbibliothek lists this publication in the Deutsche Nationalbibliografie; detailed bibliographic data are available in the Internet at http://dnb.dnb.de

ISBN 978-3-03768-157-2
© 2013 by Braun Publishing AG
www.braun-publishing.ch

1st edition 2013

Editor: Sibylle Kramer
Editorial staff and layout: Helen Gührer, Sabine Heußel, Rossella Mungari Cotruzzolà
Translation: Cosima Talhouni
Graphic concept: Michaela Prinz, Berlin
Reproduction: Bild1Druck GmbH, Berlin